Ketogenic Diet for Beginners

Simple and Fun 3 Weeks Diet Plan for the Smart

DIANA WATSON

Copyright © 2017 Diana Watson

All rights reserved.

DEDICATION

Table of Contents

Introduction

Chapter 1: How it Works

Chapter 2: All About Food

Chapter 3: Ketogenic Breakfasts

Chapter 4: Ketogenic Lunches

Chapter 5: Ketogenic

Dinners

Chapter 6: Ketogenic Snacks

Conclusion

VIP Subscriber List

Hi Dear Reader, this is Diana! If you like my book and you want to receive the latest tips and tricks on cooking, weight-loss, cookbook recipes and more, do subscribe to my mailing list in the link here! I will then be able to send you the most up-to-date information about my upcoming books and promotions as well! Thank you for supporting my work and happy reading!

Introduction

Congratulations on purchasing *Ketogenic Diet for Beginners: Simple and Fun 3 Weeks Diet Plan for the Smart* and thank you for doing so. The following chapters will discuss what exactly the ketogenic diet is and how it can help you improve your life, whether it be from weight loss or a boost in energy. The benefits of the ketogenic diet are immense, which means you too can start to make a powerful and wise lifestyle change.

There are plenty of books on this subject on the market, thanks again for choosing this one! Every effort was made to ensure it is full of as much useful information as possible, please enjoy!

Chapter 1: How It Works

There are so many different diet plans out there, it can be confusing and overwhelming when you are deciding which one would work best for you. Some of these diets are trends or fads and not something that can be maintained long-term, others might make you feel hungry all the time, which as you know, does not make for a happy life. This is one of the reasons the ketogenic diet stands apart from the rest, it will help you lose weight, while also letting you feel satisfied. You are not starving your body of calories or fat on the ketogenic diet.

What Does Ketogenic Mean?

When you eat a more traditional diet that is higher in carbohydrates your body produces glucose and insulin. Glucose is the body's first choice of energy source because it is the easiest for the body to convert. Insulin's role is to process the glucose that is in your bloodstream by taking it around the body. When this happens, it means that the fats in your body are not needed, since they are not the energy source. The fat still has to go somewhere though, so the body stores it for later use.

When you lower your carbohydrate intake, your body will enter into a state known as ketosis, which is where the word ketogenic comes from. Ketosis is what the body initiates when food consumption is low, it is a natural process that is meant to help the body survive. During ketosis the liver will break down fats and produce ketones which can also be used as fuel for the body, but only if glucose is in short supply. Remember, glucose is the body's first choice, so it will only use something else when glucose is not an option. It is not because it can't or that is not healthy, when using ketones as fuel, the body just has to work a little harder.

The goal of the ketogenic diet is to get your body to switch from using glucose as its fuel supply, to ketones, which you would get from the breakdown of fat. Therefore, your body would be getting all its energy from fat. As your insulin levels lower, your body's fat burning abilities will increase. For most people, this happens very quickly and quite dramatically. One of the benefits of this diet is how easy it becomes to burn through stored fat, which obviously helps if weight loss is your main goal.

The quickest way to enter ketosis is by fasting, however that cannot be maintained without harmful effects. The ketogenic diet can be followed indefinitely, while still allowing the body to enter ketosis. This is not a diet that deals with calorie counting, meaning you cannot eat what ever you want as long as you don't go over your caloric limit. Keeping your carbohydrate intake low, it is suggested no more than 20 or 30g of net carbohydrates is how you will be successful. However, the less you consume, the more dramatic your weight loss will be.

What is a Net Carb?

Net carb = Total dietary carbohydrate – Total fiber

Let's assume you want to eat one cup of broccoli, which contains 6g of total carbohydrates and 2g of fiber. To find the net carbs, you would then take the 6g minus the 2g, leaving you with 4g, which is the net carb amount.

Your ketogenic diet should be made of around 70 percent fats, 25 percent proteins, and only 5 percent should be carbohydrates. This is why it is so important to pay attention to what you are putting into your body and whether or not it will prevent you from entering ketosis.

The ketogenic diet will yield impressive results, but only if you stick to it. When you eat too many carbohydrates, your body will have the insulin it needs to use as fuel, meaning the fat will be stored instead of burned. The secret to a successful ketogenic diet is to plan-out what you will eat, this will not only reduce your stress, but it will also keep you on the right track.

Just like any diet or lifestyle change, it will take time for you to properly adjust to it, but you can do it.

One of the best things you can do for yourself is to keep an open mind and allow yourself the time necessary to acclimate. Rushing things before you are fully prepared will not help you, it will only cause you added stress which will probably lead to failure. To prevent this from happening, it is crucial that you find what works for you while still adhering to the diet.

Some people prefer to prep their meals a head of time, especially breakfast and lunch since they often take it with them to work. Other people like to write out their meals like a menu and stick with their ideas. You don't have to do this, but it definitely make things easier on you, especially in the beginning.

When you are on a special diet like this one, it probably won't take you very long to see how much easier it is to cook at home. Being in complete control of your food is crucial to remaining in ketosis and losing weight. That being said, if you do decide to go to a restaurant, make sure to ask any appropriate questions involving your order. Being specific about what foods are cooked in or how they are prepared will help make sure you are sticking to your diet.

Just remember, you are not going to be hungry, your body is learning to depend a different fuel for energy. That takes some time to get accustomed to, so be patient with yourself and find what works best for you. For instance, if you prefer to prep all of your meals for the week on Sunday, do it. However, if you work the night shift and enjoy cooking when you arrive home in the morning, feel free to do it that way, just find what works for you and stick to it.

Chapter 2: All About Food

Starting a new diet can be frustrating and irritating, especially if you think you are sticking to the rules, but are not seeing any positive results. This is why it is so important to know exactly what you are allowed to eat what you are not. If you don't know what foods are acceptable and are not knowledgeable about your diet, you won't be successful, regardless of the effort you are putting forth. So, make it easy on yourself and learn which foods you should eat and which you should avoid.

The best way to think of the ketogenic diet is to think real, whole foods. Anything that is prepackaged or processed is full of net carbohydrates and is off limits. This means staying away from pastas, cereals, breads, and cakes. Fruits and vegetables also contain carbohydrates so it is important that you also keep track of these net carbs as well. You already know that your diet is going to consist of mostly healthy fats, but you might understand what that means exactly. Well, first, not all fats are equal, some are definitely better for you than others and it is crucial that you know the difference.

Fats, Good and Bad

Foods contain different types of fats, but are categorized by what they contain the most of. For instance, butter is considered a saturated fat because it contains 60 percent saturated fat. As you move forward with your diet you will quickly understand the role fats play, without them you would be hungry all the time and would be left feeling unsatisfied.

Saturated Fats – These are known as essential to our health as they help to keep our immune systems healthy. In addition to helping with the immune system, this fat will also help balance hormone levels and maintain a normal bone density. This type of fat has a bad reputation and time and again has been included in the 'bad for you' category, but many different studies have shown that they are important and necessary for a healthy body. Meats, butter, and eggs all have saturated fats in them.

Polyunsaturated Fats – This is the type of fat that is commonly found in vegetable oils, and for a long time they were thought to be beneficial. However, that is not the case as they are often over processed, for instance, "heart healthy" margarines have been linked to heart disease. Yet, polyunsaturated fats that are natural such as those found in fish actually help to lower cholesterol, so it is important to know the difference and not get them confused. This is why real, natural foods are so important because the fats they contain are much better for you than their highly processed counterparts.

Monounsaturated Fats – This is an accepted healthy fat, as it improves insulin resistance and cholesterol levels. This type of fat is found in both sunflower and olive oils, both of which are common and easy to incorporate into your diet.

Trans Fats – You probably already know that trans fats are not good for you, they do not occur in natural fatty foods, only processed fatty foods. That is an important distinction, because this type of fat is created from chemicals that are used to extend a food's shelf-life. For instance, the hydrogenation process is when hydrogen is added to these fats which changes their chemical make-up. Even if a label does not say it contains trans fats, if it says hydrogenated on it, avoid it.

When you are doing your grocery shopping, try to purchase organic products and grass-fed proteins. Avoid canned or frozen fruits and vegetables too, but it is understandable that some people just do not have the financial means to do this, so be cautious and make sure you read all the labels. The next chapters are going to contain some recipes that you can try, but as you progress with your diet, you will see how easy it is to incorporate healthy fats into your meals. This will help you feel satisfied and will help you stay fuller longer.

Fats:

Avocado

Beef Tallow

Chicken Fat

Macadamia Nuts

Ghee

Butter

Non-hydrogenated Lard

Mayonnaise – read the label and make sure it does not have added carbs.

Red palm oil

Peanut butter

Olive oil

Coconut oil

Proteins:

Fish – Try to purchase wild caught if available, this can include salmon, trout, catfish, halibut, cod, flounder, mackerel, tuna, and snapper.

Shellfish – Crab, oysters, mussels, squid, lobster, scallops, and clams.

Whole Eggs – Opt for free-range if you can, local organic farmers often have them cheaper than your local grocery stores. When it comes to preparation you have many different options such as boiled, poached, scrambled, deviled, and fried.

Meat – Grass-fed typically has a higher fatty acid count, so opt for grass-fed when given the opportunity. Goat, lamb, veal, beef, and other wild game are all good choices.

Pork – You can eat nearly any type of pork, just make sure to read the label to make sure there are no added sugars.

Poultry – Pheasant, quail, chicken, and duck are all acceptable, but choose free range and organic if it is possible.

Sausage and Bacon – This can still be an acceptable and even beneficial protein as long as you choose it wisely, make sure there are no extra fillers and that it is not cured in sugar.

Peanut Butter – Choose natural peanut butter, but make sure to read the label carefully, even the most natural peanut butter can contain high amounts of carbohydrates, a better alternative is macadamia nut butter.

Vegetables

The best vegetables to eat on the ketogenic diet are those that are leafy and grow above ground. Again, if you can eat organic, try to do so as there will less pesticides used in the growing process, but if you can't try not to worry too much. Studies have shown that both non-organic and organic vegetables have the same nutritional qualities.

Of course vegetables are good for you, but some are better than others in terms of the ketogenic diet. For instance, some vegetables are high in sugar and lower in important nutrients, these are the types of vegetables that you want to either cut out altogether or consume only in very small portions. The best vegetables for this diet are those that are low in carbohydrates and high in nutrients, such as kale and anything green leafy that resembles it. These types of veggies are also easy to include in meals and they really pack a powerful nutrition punch as well.

Remember, vegetables also contain carbohydrates, so make sure you are keeping track throughout the day so you stay well within the acceptable limit. The following is a list of vegetables and their net carbohydrates by ounce.

Avocado - .6

Broccoli – 1.1

Baby Carrots – 1.5

Cauliflower - .5

Celery - .3

Cucumber – 1

Green Beans – 1.3

Mushrooms - .6

Green Onion – 1.3

White Onion – 2.1

Green Pepper - .8

Romaine Lettuce - .3

Butterhead Lettuce - .3

Shallots – 3.9

Snow Peas – 2.8

Spinach - .4

Acorn Squash – 2.9

Butternut Squash – 2.1

Spaghetti Squash – 1.4

Tomato - .8

As you begin making your own meal plans, simply add up the net carbohydrates between the different foods so you have an idea of how many you are consuming from that meal. This will get easier over time, you can even try writing it down in the beginning until you get more comfortable keeping track.

Dairy

Dairy products are also acceptable as long as there is no added sugars or other additives. It is best to go choose full fat, raw, and organic.

Sour Cream

Cottage Cheese

Heavy Whipping Cream

Hard and Soft Cheeses (Cream cheese, cheddar, mozzarella, mascarpone, etc)

You probably are guessed what is going to be said next, but it really can't be stressed enough, make sure you read the labels. Many cheeses are low in net carbohydrates as it is, but if you are in doubt either read the label or as the person behind the counter.

Nuts and Seeds

Seeds and nuts are a great way to add healthy fats to your diet and make a wonderful and convenient snack. It is best to eat them when they are roasted, this process removes any anti-nutrients. It is also important to note that there is a difference between a nut and a legume, nuts are allowed, while legumes are generally not permitted. Oddly enough, based on the name, a peanut is a legume and should be avoided. Here is a list of acceptable nuts and seeds:

Macadamias, walnuts, and almonds, all of these should be eaten in moderation, but their carbohydrate count is relatively low.

Pistachios and cashews are both higher in carbohydrates, but do contain healthy fats, so make sure you keep careful track of them.

Tip: Seed and nut flower are good alternatives to white or wheat flour, but try not to make this a staple in your diet because nuts are high in Omega-6 fatty acids, so be careful with over eating them because it can lead to weight gain and slow your progress.

Beverages

When you start your ketogenic diet, you will notice that it will have a natural diuretic effect, which means hydration is even more important. Also, if you are someone who is prone to bladder pain or urinary tract infections, you will need to be even more diligent when it comes to hydrating. It is suggested that you not only drink the recommended eight glasses of water each day, more in addition. Our bodies are made up of 2/3 water, so make sure you are keeping it happy and hydrated. Drink appropriate liquids like it is going out of style!

Water, drink it. Drink a lot of it.

Coffee, with heavy cream and no sugar, it is fine in moderation.

Tea, also no added sugar and if you like it with milk make sure it is raw and whole fat or use heavy cream.

Sweeteners

Of course it is best to avoid anything that is sweet, but for some of us with a sweet tooth, this would just make us miserable. That being said, if you have a sweet craving that you can't seem to deny, choose an artificial sweetener and try not to do this often. Liquid sweeteners are better since there are no added binders like in the powder forms that have carbohydrates.

Stevia

Sucralose

Monk Fruit

Erythirol

Xylitol

Spices

When it comes to what you eat, you want it to be flavorful and satisfying, most of which will come from the addition of spices. However, many spices contain carbohydrates, so it is important that you keep track of the amounts of you are using and add those amounts to your carbohydrate total for your meal. You can use nearly any dry spices you prefer, just make sure you look up the carbohydrate content, no one wants your food to be boring and bland. Some spices have more carbs than others, such as cinnamon, garlic powder, allspice, bay leaves, ginger, and cardamom, so if those are staples in your cooking, make sure you are keeping accurate track.

Watch Out For

Fruit – Limit your fruit content because fruit is high in natural sugars and therefore carbohydrates. Many people use berries in desserts or as snacks, but only in small portions and not very often. If you choose to do this, be cautious of raspberries, cranberries, and blueberries.

Tomato – Food companies are very good at making their products look healthier than they really are. Tomatoes do have natural sugars in them, but when you buy tomato based products additional sugar is often added. That doesn't mean you can't use canned tomato sauces or diced tomatoes, just make sure you read the labels.

Peppers – Most of us do not think of peppers as being full of sugars, green has the last amount of sugars compared to red or yellow.

Diet Sodas – You can still drink diet soda, just pay

close attention to how much you are drinking and try to limit yourself if you are soda dependent. Some people have reported that they were knocked out of ketosis from consuming too much artificial sweetener, so just keep that in mind when you are considering a diet soda.

Salt – Since the ketogenic diet acts as a natural diuretic, you will see that your body does not retain salt the same way it did before. This means that salt and other electrolytes are flushed from the body very quickly, this can lead to many different health issues such as panic attacks and heart palpitations. To prevent this from happening you can include salted bone broth into your diet or you can use what is known as a light salt that is a combination of both salt and potassium. Most people also choose to take a supplement for anything they think are not getting enough of from their diet.

Water – When you think you have consumed enough water, drink a little more. Your body is going through some huge changes and part of that is flushing out liquids faster than before, so to keep yourself healthy it is a good idea to drink water, a lot of water.

In The Beginning

If this your first time embarking on a low carbohydrate diet, there are some things you need to know. Your body is doing to go through what is known as detox symptoms, this is perfectly natural, but uncomfortable. Remember, you are retraining your body, that doesn't happen without consequences. However, don't be discouraged, they only last for a few days and no matter how bad it feels, you can and will get through it.

These withdrawal symptoms are commonly referred to as the "keto flu," which sounds much worse than it is. Just keep telling yourself that the first three days are the hardest and it will get much easier after. Here is a list of the symptoms:

Irritability

Fatigue

Dizziness

Intense Cravings

Basically, your body is acting like an unruly child who wants sugar, because it has become so accustomed to it. For those who are transitioning from a very carbohydrate dense diet the symptoms will be much worse than others, it just depends on the person's body. Just don't give up. There are some things you can do to help cope with the negative side effects by increasing your water intake. When the very intense cravings hit, and they will, give your body something to eat, just not what it wants, try bacon or cheese. You are not denying yourself food, just distracting it from craving carbohydrates, until you adjust, distraction is the key to success.

Benefits

Now that you just read about the negative side effects, you might be feeling even more overwhelmed than before. However, the benefits of the ketogenic diet far outweighs the negative. Here is a list of the benefits:

Less appetite - After your body has had time to adjust to ketosis, your appetite will just naturally be reduced. This will also eventually lead to less calorie intake too.

Weight Loss - Not only will you lose weight on this diet, but not all fat is the same. When you hold more fat in the abdominal area, this can cause many different health issues, even increasing your risk of heart disease. The ketogenic diet will help you lose weight in the abdominal area, and usually rather quickly, this will help those who are risk for type 2 diabetes as well as heart disease.

Blood Pressure - The ketogenic diet helps to reduce high blood pressure and is often suggested by doctors for this reason.

The Brain - Some parts of the brain can only use glucose which is why our liver will create glucose from protein when we do not eat carbohydrates. However, most of the brain is capable of using ketones as fuel. Allowing the brain to use ketones as fuel has helped many children and adults alike with epilepsy. Currently, scientists are looking into a connection between the ketogenic diet and Alzheimer's disease.

Now, you have an idea of what you are going to be eating and how to count the net carbohydrates in the foods. When you first start out, keep very close track of your portion sizes so you can keep an accurate record of the net carbs. If you are choosing to remain under 20 net carbohydrates a day, then make sure to include not only the ingredients from the meal you are eating, but also from the beverage and even the spices. You will want to do this for each meal so you know for sure you are not exceeding your limit.

This is probably not going to come very easily in the beginning, but rest assured, it will get easier for you. Also, after you stick to the diet for a couple of weeks, you will already start to see results and nothing works to motivate quite like seeing the desired results. Even if it feels like you just can't keep going, or you want to give up, don't, it was hard for nearly everyone in the beginning. You are going through something huge, retraining your brain and learning to control your cravings. Chances are, you are also breaking some bad habits as well, so give yourself the necessary time to fully adjust.

Chapter 3
Ketogenic Breakfasts

This is a collection of ketogenic recipes that you can mix and match to give you a three week jump start on your diet. This will help you by taking the guess work out of what to make and it will also give you a general idea of how to prepare the correct foods for yourself. Once you start your new diet, you might find that you choose to meal prep for the week, and if that is the case, make sure your choices are able to be stored appropriately.

Many people think breakfast is one of the hardest meals to create because you can only eat so many eggs and bacon before you are craving variety. For that purpose, traditional eggs and bacon or sausage are going to be avoided, in favor of other easy and more creative options.

Egg Porridge

1/3 cup heavy cream

2 eggs

Cinnamon to taste

2 tablespoons butter

Berries, optional

Sweetener, optional

This is a ketogenic version of oatmeal or porridge, it is based on how eggs curdle and uses that grainy feel as added texture. You can choose whether or not to add berries or sweetener, depending on how many carbohydrates you are allotting yourself.

1. Combine the cream, eggs, and sweetener if you choose to use it in a small bowl and whisk the mixture together until uniform in color.
2. In a saucepan melt the butter over medium-high heat, but keep an eye on it and do not allow it to turn brown. Once the butter is melted, turn the heat to low.
3. Add the cream and egg mixture to the butter in the saucepan, make sure you continue mixing, especially along the bottom because that is where it will start to curdle and thicken first. Once you start to see the little grains or curdles remove it from the heat.
4. Add a serving to a bowl and sprinkle the top with cinnamon and the berries if you choose.

Cream Cheese Pancakes

2 eggs

½ teaspoon cinnamon

2 ounces of cream cheese (read the label and make sure there are no added sugars)

1 teaspoon sweetener, optional

Butter, to grease pan

You will also need a blender or a food processor for this recipe.

1. Place all the ingredients into the blender or food processor and mix until smooth. Sit it aside and allow it to rest for two or three minutes, or until the bubbles are settled.
2. Grease the pan and set it on medium high heat, with the butter and pour the batter onto the pan, just like you would with traditional pancakes. Cook for two minutes and then flip, cook for an additional minute or until golden brown. Repeat this until all of the batter has been used.
3. You can eat these with sugar-free syrup, berries, or nothing at all depending on what your carbohydrate limit is.

This is a great recipe to make for large groups since it is so easy and quick. They will make a great addition to your diet and will leave you feeling full and satisfied.

Lemon Poppy Seed Muffins

2 tablespoons poppy seeds

Zest of 2 lemons

3 tablespoons lemon juice

3 large eggs

¾ cup almond flour

¼ cup flaxseed meal

1 teaspoon vanilla extract

¼ cup heavy cream

1/3 cup erythritol

1 teaspoon baking powder

¼ salted butter, melted

25 drops of liquid sweetener

Muffin pan and liners

1. Set your oven to 250F, and in a bowl combine the flaxseed meal, poppy seeds, almond flour, and erythritol.
2. Slowly pour in the eggs and heavy cream, stir constantly until the mixture is smooth and there are no lumps in the batter.
3. Once the mixture is smooth add the sweetener, vanilla extract, lemon juice, lemon zest, and baking powder. Make sure to stir this well to ensure everything is mixed together properly.
4. Put your liners in the muffin pan, or silicone molds, this batter will make 12 muffins, but if you need to you can adjust the size a little, just try not to make them too big.
5. Place your batter in the oven and bake for 18 to 20 minutes, if you want a crispier crust on the bottom, leave them in for a bit longer.

6. When they are finished baking, take them out of the oven and let them rest on the counter for around 10 minutes.

These are the perfect breakfast for people who want something they can easily take with them. If you know you are in for a busy week, these make for a great breakfast to make before your work week starts.

'McGriddle' Casserole

10 eggs

1 cup almond flour

¼ cup flaxseed meal

1 pound breakfast sausage

½ teaspoon onion powder

½ teaspoon garlic powder

¼ teaspoon sage

4 tablespoons sage

4 ounce cheddar cheese

6 tablespoons sugar free syrup

Salt and pepper to taste

Casserole pan

Parchment paper

1. Preheat the oven to 350F and put a pan on medium heat, this is for the breakfast sausage. You are going to break it up as you brown it.
2. In a large mixing bowl combine all of the dry ingredients, mix them together and then add the wet ingredients, but only put in 4 tablespoons of the syrup. Mix everything together until is uniform and smooth.

3. After your mixture is mixed well, add the cheese and stir some more.
4. Throughout this process, you should also be checking on your sausage to make sure it is not getting too brown, you just want it to be a little crispy. When it is cooked to your liking, pour it, with the fat, into the mixture and stir everything together.
5. Place the parchment paper into your casserole pan and pour the mixture into the dish. Drizzle the remaining syrup over the top of the mixture.
6. Bake for about 45 to 55 minutes, if your pan is larger and your casserole thinner, you will need to adjust the cooking time to a bit less. You want the inside to be cooked through completely though, you'll know it is when it is golden brown and looks firm.
7. When it is done cooking, remove it from the oven and gently pull out the parchment paper, slice the casserole into pieces and serve with either sugar-free ketchup, or even a little more syrup.

This is a great recipe that you can eat all week. Feel free to alter the recipe to suit your needs, for instance, if you think it is too much syrup, you can adjust the amount.

Breakfast Tacos

6 eggs

3 strips of bacon

½ avocado

1 cup shredded mozzarella, make sure it is whole milk

1 ounce shredded cheddar cheese

2 tablespoons butter

Salt and pepper to taste

1. First, you are going to cook the bacon, the easiest way is to preheat your oven to 375F and bake it for 15 to 20 minutes, but if you choose to cook it in a pan, that's fine too.
2. While the bacon is cooking, put 1/3 of a cup of mozzarella in a clean pan on medium heat. You want it to be uniform in thickness and in a circle, this is what will be your taco shell. Be patient, this takes some practice to get right, but you'll get the hang of it.
3. After about two or three minutes the edges will be brown, this is when you are going to carefully slide a spatula underneath it. If you used whole milk mozzarella this should be easy since the oils in it prevent it from sticking naturally.
4. Rest a wooden spoon over a large bowl, using either tongs or your spatula, gently drape the mozzarella over the spoon so as it hardens it will be in the shape of a crunchy taco shell. Do this to the rest of the mozzarella, which will leave you with three completed shells when finished.

5. Your next step is to cook your eggs in the butter, you can do a soft or a hard scramble, it's your preference.
6. When your eggs are finished, spoon them into each of your taco shells and add the sliced avocado on top. Then top with our bacon, you can simply place the entire slice on each, or dice it up.
7. The final step is to sprinkle the cheddar cheese on each taco and enjoy.

This is a breakfast that helps people transition when they are craving that crunch that carbohydrates provides. So, if you find yourself craving chips or breads, this might help satisfy you. Keep in mind though, that even though these do not take too long to make, they are not like the casserole where you can make extra for the week. You are pretty much just making a serving at a time.

Brownie Muffins

¼ cup cocoa powder

1 cup flaxseed meal

½ tablespoon baking powder

1 egg

1 tablespoon cinnamon

2 tablespoons coconut oil

½ teaspoon salt

½ can pumpkin puree

¼ tsp sugar-free caramel syrup

1 teaspoon apple cider vinegar

¼ cup slivered almonds

1 teaspoon vanilla extract

1. Preheat your oven to 350F and put all the dry ingredients into a large mixing bowl.

2. In a separate mixing bowl combine all the wet ingredients and stir until uniform and smooth.
3. Gently pour the wet ingredients into the dry bowl and mix together until everything is smooth and it is smooth.
4. Put your muffin liners into your pan and spoon about ¼ cup of batter into each one, and sprinkle the almonds over the top, press them down slightly so they don't fall off. This recipe will make 6 muffins, if you need 12, simply double all of the ingredients.
5. Place them in the oven and check on them after about 15 minutes, you will know they're done when they rise. You can eat them either cold or warm, they make the perfect addition to your morning coffee.

This is the perfect breakfast for anyone who has a sweet tooth. So, for those who are starting a low carbohydrate diet for the first time, these can help with those intense sweet carb cravings. You should not feel hungry and unsatisfied on your diet and this is a great way to make sure that doesn't happen.

These breakfasts can be mixed and matched throughout the weeks, or you can make the casserole and eat it for the whole week. You can even freeze individual servings and microwave it when needed. You want your diet to work around your life, not change your life to work around your diet. Too many huge changes at one time can lead to failure. So, find what meals work for you and stick to it, for instance, if you are more likely to hit the snooze button on your alarm and find yourself rushing, setting aside time to cook an elaborate breakfast, might not be feasible. If that is the case, the casserole or the muffins would be best for you.

Chapter 4
Ketogenic Lunches

When it comes to ketogenic friendly foods, it is usually best if you prepare them at home so you know exactly what you're eating. If you have a tendency to go out to lunch when you are at work, bringing it might seem strange in the beginning.

However, it is easier than trying to find ketogenic friendly foods on a menu that does not usually have them specifically listed. Going out to eat can be frustrating because you will need to ask the server so many different questions about ingredients. Until you are more comfortable and confident with your diet, it is a good idea to bring your lunch with you, just to ensure that you remain in ketosis.

Just like with the breakfasts, you can make your lunches daily if you choose, or you can prep things a head of time. Some people prefer to only make lunches that can frozen in individual servings so all they have to do is thrown the Tupperware into their lunchbox and be on their way. Others prefer to prepare their lunch night before or their morning of work, depending on time and what they are in the mood for. The following recipes are all easy and quick, and fit well with the mix and match three week plan.

Mixed Green Salad

3 tablespoons roasted pine nuts

2 tablespoons shaved parmesan

2 ounces of mixed greens

2 slices of bacon

Salt and pepper to taste

Ketogenic friendly dressing of your choice, read the label carefully

1. Cook the bacon until it is crispy, you can do this the oven or in a pan, it is up to you. Some people prefer to burn the edges just a bit to add bitter notes to the salad, this complements vinaigrette dressings especially well.
2. Put your portioned greens into a container that has a lid with some extra room, this is for shaking purposes, so keep that in mind when choosing.
3. Crumble the bacon into the greens and toss in the rest of the ingredients including the dressing. Put the lid on the top and shake the

container until the dressing coats the greens evenly.

If you are taking this with you to work, wait until you get to work to combine the ingredients. You can keep them separate in reusable bags or in small containers. This helps to keep the salad from getting soggy.

Pigs in a Keto Blanket

37 small sausages, read the label carefully

1 egg

1.5 ounces of cream cheese

8 ounces of cheddar cheese

¾ almond flour

1 tablespoon psyllium husk powder, or coconut flour

Salt and pepper to taste

1. Combine all the dry ingredients in a large bowl.
2. Melt the cheddar cheese in 20 second intervals in the microwave, stir carefully to ensure it is melting evenly. It is done when it is completely melted and slightly bubbling on the outside.
3. Mix together all the ingredients while the cheddar is still hot, this will be your dough.
4. Spread the dough out in a flat and even sheet, make sure it is not too thick, you have 37 sausages to cover after all.
5. Preheat your oven to 400F and put the dough in the refrigerator for 15 to 20 minutes to let it harden up a bit.
6. Once it is cold, slice the dough into strips, a pizza cutter is perfect for this, and wrap them around the sausages. Put them in the oven and bake them for 13 to 15 minutes, before you remove them, broil them for an additional one or two minutes.

These make a great lunch because they can be reheated once you get to work. You can eat them with a sugar-free ketchup or mustard if you choose. In addition to making a convenient lunch, these also make the perfect snack to bring to a party. When you go to gatherings or parties you might find that there is a lack of ketogenic snacks. Unless otherwise specified, it is safe to assume that you might be faced with a table full of foods you can't eat. The easy solution is to bring your own, these are perfect for that.

Tuna Melt Balls with Avocado

10 ounce canned tuna, drained

1 avocado

1/3 cup almond flour

¼ cup mayonnaise, read the label to check for

added sugars

¼ cup parmesan cheese

¼ teaspoon onion powder

½ teaspoon garlic powder

Salt and pepper to taste

½ coconut oil for frying, approximately a ¼ cup will be absorbed

1. Drain the tuna and put it a bowl that is large enough to hold all of the ingredients.
2. Add the parmesan cheese, spices, and mayonnaise to the tuna and mix it together until evenly coated.
3. Slice your avocado in half and carefully take out the pit, cube the inside. If you have a way that you prefer to cut avocados, feel free to do what makes you comfortable, just make sure the pieces are in small cubes.
4. Add the avocado in with the rest of the mixture, but fold it in slowly, try not to mash it too much, you want pieces to remain.

5. Roll the mixture into balls, about the size of traditional meat balls. Then roll them in the almond flour, make sure they are evenly coated.
6. Put the coconut oil in a pan on medium heat, when it is hot add the tuna balls and fry them until they are brown and crisp on the outside. Make sure you are turning them to ensure each side is cooked properly.
7. Now, simply remove from the pan and serve.

These are a great ketogenic version of a tuna melt, you get the creamy center and the added crunch of the outside. Granted, they are not going to be as crunchy when they are reheated, but they are still delicious and easy to take to work with you.

Pizza Frittata

9 ounce bag frozen spinach

12 eggs

1 ounce pepperoni

1 teaspoon minced garlic

5 ounce mozzarella cheese

½ cup parmesan cheese

½ cup fresh ricotta cheese

4 tablespoons olive oil

¼ teaspoon nutmeg

Salt and pepper to taste

Iron skillet or glass container

1. Microwave the frozen spinach for three to four minutes, you don't want to be hot, just defrosted. Then squeeze the spinach with your hands to remove as much water as you can and then set it aside.
2. Preheat your oven to 375F and while it is getting hot, mix together the olive oil, eggs, and spices. Stir or whisk this together until everything is combined.
3. Break the spinach up into small pieces and toss it in the mixture. Next, add the parmesan and ricotta cheeses and mix everything together until it is well combined.
4. Pour your mixture into the skillet and then cover with the mozzarella, place the pepperoni on top just like you would a traditional pizza.
5. Put in the oven and bake for 30 minutes if you are using the cast iron skillet, add an additional 10 to 15 minutes if it is glass. You might need to adjust the baking time depending on the thickness of the frittata, but you will know when it is done when it is slightly browned and firm.

6. Then, just slice and serve.

This a perfect lunch to make at the beginning of the week, that will provide enough servings to last the entire week. It is easy to bring to work and once you are there, you can simply heat it up.

Chicken and BBQ Soup

Base

2 teaspoons chili seasoning

3 chicken thighs

1 ½ cups chicken broth

2 tablespoons of olive oil or chicken fat

1 ½ cups of beef broth

Salt and pepper to taste

Sauce

1 tablespoon hot sauce

¼ cup reduced sugar ketchup

2 tablespoons Dijon mustard

¼ cup tomato paste

1 teaspoon Worcestershire sauce

2 1.2 teaspoon liquid smoke

1 tablespoon soy sauce

1 teaspoon onion powder

1 teaspoon red chili flakes

1 teaspoon chili powder

1 teaspoon cumin

¼ cup butter

1 ½ teaspoons garlic powder

Crock pot or slow cooker

1. Preheat the oven to 400F and remove the bones from the chicken thighs and keep the bones. Season the chicken with some of the chili seasoning and put on a baking tray that is lined with foil.
2. Place the chicken in the oven and bake for 50 minutes.
3. While the chicken is in the oven, grab a pot and add the chicken fat or olive oil, heat this on medium high heat and when it is hot put the chicken bones into the oil and cook them for five minutes. Next, add the broth and season with salt and pepper to taste.
4. When the chicken is done baking, take them out and remove the skins and set aside. Pour the fat from the baked chicken into the broth, stirring occasionally.

5. Now you are going to BBQ sauce by combining all of the ingredients listed above. Then add it to the large pot and stir everything together. Let the mixture simmer for about 20 to 30 minutes.
6. After it has had time to simmer, use an immersion blender, this will emulsify the liquids and fats together. Shred the chicken and put it in the soup, you can also add bell pepper or spring onions during this step if you choose to and simmer for another 10 to 20 minutes.
7. After it has had time to thicken up, you can now serve it up. You can garnish it with a little cheddar cheese, onions, or some diced up green peppers. The crispy chicken you set aside should also be served on the side as well, it makes a great texture addition to the meal.

This is a great lunch option because you can put individual servings in plastic containers and either refrigerate or freeze them for later use. Then when you need a quick lunch on the go, grab the container, throw it your lunch box and be on your way. If that works better for you, than you should really consider utilizing more recipes like these.

Grilled Cheese Keto Style

'Bread'

2 tablespoons almond flour

2 eggs

1 ½ tablespoons psyllium husk powder

2 tablespoons soft butter

½ teaspoon baking powder

Extras

1 tablespoon butter, soft

2 ounces of white or traditional cheddar

1. Combine the butter, almond flour, baking powder, and psyllium husk in a small bowl.
2. Stir this mixture together as much as you can, it will take the form of a very thick dough.
3. Add the 2 eggs and mix it together, you want your dough to be thick, so it seems too thin, keep mixing it together, as this will help thicken it up. This can take a full minute or more so be patient.
4. Scoop half the dough out into a square container roughly the size of a slice of bread, or the bottom a bowl to create bun, try to make sure it is spread evenly. You can also use a slightly larger container and cut in half later, if that is what you choose to do, use all the batter. Microwave this for a 90 to 100 seconds. Some might take a little longer to cook thoroughly so check it and it if it still too soft, microwave it for a little longer.
5. Gently remove it from the container by turning it upside down and tapping on the bottom of

the container. If you used all of your batter you can cut it in half, if you need to repeat the process to create the other slice of bread, then do so.
6. Place the cheese in between the slices of bread.
7. In a pan set on medium heat add the butter and when it is hot add the sandwich. The bread will absorb the butter creating that delicious crisp, once it is golden brown, flip and cook the other side until golden brown.
8. Lastly, it is time to eat! A small side salad makes the perfect addition to this gooey, cheesy dish.

This is a great comfort food and probably one of the things that you will find yourself craving rather frequently. Again, just because you are on the ketogenic diet does not mean you have to give up everything you love, you just need to learn to make it in new and different ways that won't compromise ketosis.

Remember, this is a mix and match meal plan, you do not have to eat all the meals, but do try to keep an open mind. There is no lack of variety when it comes to the ketogenic diet, as a matter of fact, you can still have many of the foods you crave, they will just have a bit of a twist added to them. Whether or not you choose to make your lunches for the whole week or that day is up to you, but you do have the option. Keep in mind, this will get much easier the more you practice. In the beginning, the key is planning and sticking to it. If you need to create a weekly menu to keep you on track, then do it, there is nothing wrong with it. This is your diet and you have the right to do what works for you.

Chapter 5
Ketogenic Dinners

When it comes to dinners you can be a bit more creative because there isn't typically the need to grab it and go. Most people have more time to cook a dinner and not have to worry about making enough for a full week or whether or not it will travel well. Just like with the other recipes, you are going to choose your ingredients and keep track of the net carbohydrates you are consuming and since this is the last meal of the day, you will have a good idea of how many net carbohydrates you have let to devote to your dinner.

If you have a big dinner planned that you will use up more of your net carbohydrates than usual, make sure to limit your other meals and snacks throughout the day to give yourself the surplus you need for the special dinner. Try not to make this a habit, but everyone has some type of special occasion that requires a more elaborate dinner and this is still possible on the ketogenic diet, it just takes some extra planning. Here is a list of dinner recipes that are perfect for a ketogenic beginner.

Chicken with Creamy Greens

1 cup chicken stock

1 pound boneless chicken thighs, with skin still on

1 cup cream

2 cups dark leafy greens

2 tablespoons coconut oil

2 tablespoons coconut flour

2 tablespoons melted butter

1 teaspoon Italian herbs

Salt and pepper to taste

1. In a skillet set on medium high heat add the coconut oil. While this is getting hot, season the chicken with the salt and pepper, make sure to do both sides. When the oil is hot enough, brown the chicken on both sides
2. Continue to fry the chicken until it is crispy and cooked thoroughly. When you are cooking the chicken, you should also start making your sauce.
3. In a sauce pan melt the butter, when it stops sizzling, this means do not let it get brown, only melted, add the coconut flour and begin to whisk it together. Continue to whisk until it forms a thick paste.
4. Add the cream and increase the heat to bring it to a boil, continue to whisk. It will begin to thicken again and when it does, add the Italian herbs.
5. When your chicken is done frying, remove them from the stove and take out the thighs and set them aside.
6. Add the chicken stock into the skillet that just had the chicken in it and deglaze the skillet,

slowly add the cream sauce and whisk. Slowly stir the greens into the sauce so they become evenly coated with the sauce.
7. Place the chicken on top of the greens and remove from the stove. You can now serve the meal, when dividing, it makes four servings.

Walnut Crusted Salmon

2 tablespoons sugar-free maple syrup

2, 3 ounce salmon fillets

½ cup walnuts

1 tablespoon olive oil

¼ teaspoon dill

½ tablespoon Dijon mustard

Salt and pepper to taste

1. Preheat oven to 350F.
2. Put all the walnuts in a food processor with the spices, mustard, and maple syrup. Blend this together until the consistency is very paste like.
3. In a skillet or pan heat up the olive oil until it is very hot, while this is happening dry both sides of the salmon, make sure to a do a good job. When the pan is very hot place the salmon in the pan skin down. Allow it to sear for three minutes.
4. While it searing, spoon the walnut mixture onto the fillets.

5. When they have finished being seared, place them on a pan or foil and place them in the oven to bake for around 8 minutes.
6. This is typically served on a bed of fresh spinach, but if you prefer other leafy greens, the choice is yours.

This is a quick and delicious dinner that will leave you feeling satisfied.

Crispy Baked Chicken Wings

3 pounds of wings

1 teaspoon baking soda

¼ cup of butter

1 tablespoon salt

2 teaspoons of baking powder

1. In a large plastic bag, dump in the salt, baking powder, baking soda, and all of the chicken wings.

2. Then shake the bag until all of the wings are coated in the mixture, try to make sure it is as even as possible.
3. Put all of the wings on a wire rack and leave in the refrigerator overnight, this will help them dry out which breaks the peptide bonds in the proteins.
4. The next day, preheat your oven to 450F and place the wings in the top middle rack, bake these for 20 minutes.
5. After the first 20 minutes, flip each wing over and bake for an additional 15 minutes or until they are as crispy as you like the,
6. To make a quick buffalo sauce mix together butter and hot sauce and toss them in this to make ketogenic buffalo wings. Enjoy!

This is a great dinner for when you have been watching your friends get their favorite wings from the local spot. When the craving for this type of comfort food hits you, now you can also enjoy them as well.

Stuffed Poblanos

1 tablespoon bacon fat

1 pound ground pork

½ onion

4 poblano peppers

7 baby bella mushrooms

1 teaspoon cumin

1 vine tomato

1 teaspoon chili powder

¼ cup chopped cilantro

Salt and pepper to taste

1. Rinse and prep all the vegetables, you want to mince garlic, slice the mushrooms and onions,

and dice the tomatoes. If your cilantro is not already chopped, do this as well.
2. Set your oven to broil, while this is heating up, place the poblanos on a cookie sheet and put them in the oven when it is hot. Broil them for around 8 to 10 minutes, make sure to move them around every two minutes, you want consistent marks over the entire pepper. Then preheat your oven to 350F.
3. Using a paper towel or gloves to cover your fingers, carefully pull the skin from the peppers. Also, set the skin aside.
4. In a pan that is set on medium high-heat, begin to cook the pork, this is also where you add the bacon fat. Season with salt and pepper, but do not taste it until it has cooked all the way.
5. When it is browned you may now add the chili powder and cumin.
6. In the pan, slide all of the pork to one side and add the garlic and onions to the other side, you want them to be softened.

7. When those have softened add the mushrooms and mix all of it together, add more salt and pepper to suit your palate.
8. When the mixture starts to dry out a little add the tomatoes and cilantro.
9. Make a slice in the poblano pepper from the bottom to the stem and use a spoon or your fingers to remove the seeds. The seeds are spicy, so if you are sensitive to spicy foods, be sure to remove all of them.
10. Carefully fill each pepper with the pork mixture and bake them for around 8 to 10 minutes.
11. Remove them from the oven and they are now ready to serve!

These make a unique and fun dinner for what you are craving something simple and spicy. They will probably become a staple in your new diet if you enjoy spicier foods.

Coconut Shrimp

Shrimp

Egg whites from two eggs

1 pound shrimp, deveined and peeled

2 tablespoons coconut flour

1 cup coconut flakes, unsweetened

Chili Sauce

1 ½ tablespoon rice wine vinegar

1 diced red chili

½ cup apricot preserves, sugar-free

¼ red pepper flakes

1 tablespoon lime juice

1. If you are using frozen shrimp, make sure you thaw them out first, otherwise, if you bought them fresh peel and devein them if needed. Preheat your oven to 375F.
2. Put the egg whites in a bowl and beat them until soft peaks begin to form, this works best using a hand mixer, or if you are in a pinch, one beater inside a blender also works too.

3. In one bowl put the coconut flakes, in another the coconut flour. Take this time to also grease a cookie sheet.
4. Dip the shrimp in the flour, then dip them in the egg whites, and lastly, the flakes. Arrange them on the greased cookie sheet and bake them for about 15 minutes, make sure to flip them and broil for 3 to 5 more minutes.
5. To make the sauce simply add all the ingredients into a bowl mix them together. You might have some left over sauce, but it also goes well with chicken!

These are a great alternative to chicken nuggets or fried shrimp.

Dinners are generally the most fun part of ketogenic cooking because you can really experiment to find what pleases your palate. There are so many different recipes out there already, and you can tweak them so they work for your specific diet needs. Just remember, it might be overwhelming and difficult in the beginning, but you can do it. Just don't give up, let your body adjust and celebrate the small victories like the first pound lost or the first time you didn't have a carb craving all day. This will make the diet more fun and will help keep you motivated.

Chapter 6

Ketogenic Snacks

You are not locked in to only eating three meals a day with no snacking in between. Actually, you can graze a bit throughout the day if that works for you. However, not all snacks are created equal and some are much better than others. Just make sure not to let snacking get out of hand to the point that you are knocked out of ketosis because of it. Don't forget to add in the net carbohydrates from any of the snacks you have eaten throughout the day too, you want an authentic carbohydrate count and this will help make sure it is correct.

The best kind of snacks are the ones that you do not

have to spend time preparing, and even though the ketogenic diet is best when you cook at home, there are some things that you can still just grab.

Ketogenic Snacks

Beef, pork, or chicken jerky

String Cheese

Seeds, sunflower, pumpkin, and chia

Pork rinds, just make sure to read the label, you can even dip them in ketogenic friendly dips such as Ranch or Bleu Cheese dressings.

Nut Butters, almond, coconut, and sunflower

Sugar-free jello

Cocoa nibs, this is the perfect alternative to a chocolate bar

In the beginning you might find yourself losing energy or getting hungry at weird times of the day, remember your body is learning to run on something new. So, this is completely normal. These snacks are easy to keep on hand and require no preparation. Just make sure to add them into your daily carbohydrate intake and they should help you during your transition to a low carbohydrate lifestyle.

It probably seems like this diet is overwhelming, but as soon as you get through the first couple of weeks and see the results, you will understand how beneficial it can really be. It will be difficult in the beginning, but you can and should stick it out. You will be proud of yourself in the end. So many people just like you have lost weight and enjoyed healthier lifestyles because of this diet. You don't want to let them reap all the benefits. So, don't let you, hold you back. The secret is finding what works for you and sticking to it, everyone works at their own pace and you are no exception. No matter how badly you might want to compare yourself to others, don't do it. Let your body go at the pace it is meant to, you will learn to know when it is okay to push yourself and when you have truly met your limits, but you won't know either of these until you dedicate yourself and actually try.

Conclusion

Thank for making it through to the end of *Ketogenic Diet for Beginners: Simple and Fun 3 Weeks Diet Plan for the Smart*, let's hope it was informative and able to provide you with all of the tools you need to achieve your goals whatever it may be.

The next step is to start making your meal plans and figuring out how to make the diet work the best for you.

VIP Subscriber List

Hi Dear Reader, this is Diana! If you like my book and you want to receive the latest tips and tricks on cooking, weight-loss, cookbook recipes and more, do subscribe to my mailing list in the link here! I will then be able to send you the most up-to-date information about my upcoming books and promotions as well! <u>Thank you for supporting my work and happy reading!</u>

www.ingramcontent.com/pod-product-compliance
Lightning Source LLC
LaVergne TN
LVHW010410070526
838199LV00065B/5931